Chasing Par

Written by Christa Tarr

Illustrated by Gaby Martínez Huesca

Halo
PUBLISHING INTERNATIONAL

Halo Publishing International
7550 W IH-10 #800, PMB 2069,
San Antonio, TX 78229

First Edition, November 2024
ISBN: 978-1-63765-666-2
Library of Congress Control Number: 2024917423

Halo Publishing International is a self-publishing company that publishes adult fiction and non-fiction, children's literature, self-help, spiritual, and faith-based books. Do you have a book idea you would like us to consider publishing? Please visit www.halopublishing.com for more information.

To my husband, who leads, loves, serves, and sacrifices for us unconditionally and without expectation. Thank you for pushing me to chase my dreams and for always seeing the best in me. Words will never adequately express my love, respect, and appreciation for you. You and me, always and forever.

To my daughter, who is my inspiration. Being your mom brings me infinite joy. Our countless hours reading books together have encouraged me to bring this one to life. I thank God every day for you and am blessed beyond measure to be your mama. You are my sunshine and a light in this world—keep shining brightly. And always remember to "keep your eye on the ball."

To my parents, who have always done everything you could to help me achieve my goals. Thank you for encouraging and supporting my love of the game over the years. Thank you for who you are and for all that you do for us. You're still making dreams come true.

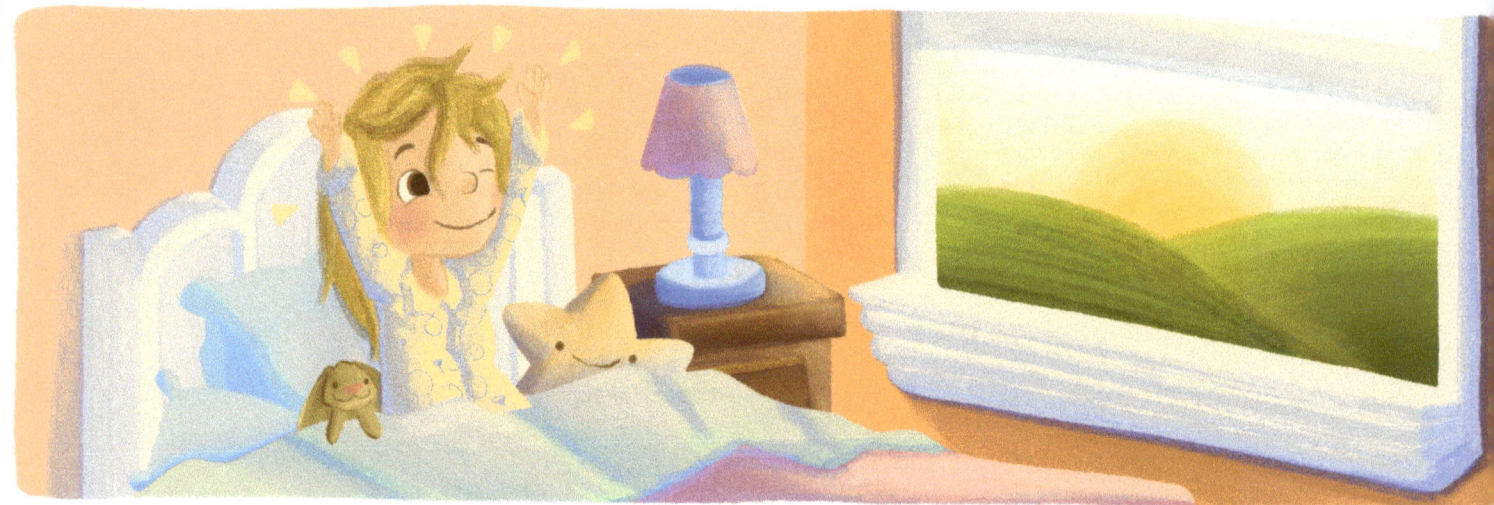

4

Ella wakes up excited.
Today is the day.
The sun is still rising.
She's ready to play.

It's her first round of golf.
She's practiced with zeal.
Ella jumps out of bed
and lets out a squeal.

It's time to get dressed,
grab breakfast and snacks.
Load up her golf clubs.
The car is all packed.

She greets her friend Leo.
He gets to play, too.
They're both chasing par.
Oh, what a great crew!

They arrive at the course,
all surrounded by green.
They unload their gear
and take in the whole scene.

Mom says, "Come on,"
grabs her clubs with a grin.
"Let's head to the pro shop.
It's time to check in!

"Then off to practice.
We need to warm up,
hit balls at the range,
and roll a few putts."

8

8

Ella swings each club,
from driver to irons.
She never knows which
a shot will require.

She hears the starter
call from under the tree,
"Your foursome is next.
Please head up to the tee!"

"Jump in the carts,"
Daddy says. "Time to go!
We need to be timely.
Get this show on the road!"

On hole number one,
Mom and Dad hit great shots.
No mulligans here.
They're both in good spots.

Leo's up next.
He hits a long drive.
It's now Ella's turn.
The time has arrived!

She's nervous but thrilled
while grabbing her driver.
"Just do what you've practiced,"
Daddy kindly reminds her.

She takes a deep breath
and tees up her ball.
"Have fun, and swing smooth!"
Ella hears Mommy call.

She brings the club back,
stays down, and swings through.
"Just like that!" Leo roars.
"See what you can do!"

It went straight down the fairway.
That's a great start!
Ella skips to her ball
with a full, pounding heart.

She aims to get close
to the pin on the green.
She takes an iron,
but she hurries her swing.

Oh no! It sliced right,
straight into the sand.
Really, that's golf, though.
Not all goes as planned.

Her friend says, "Don't worry
about what went wrong.
Bad shots will happen.
Stay calm and swing on."

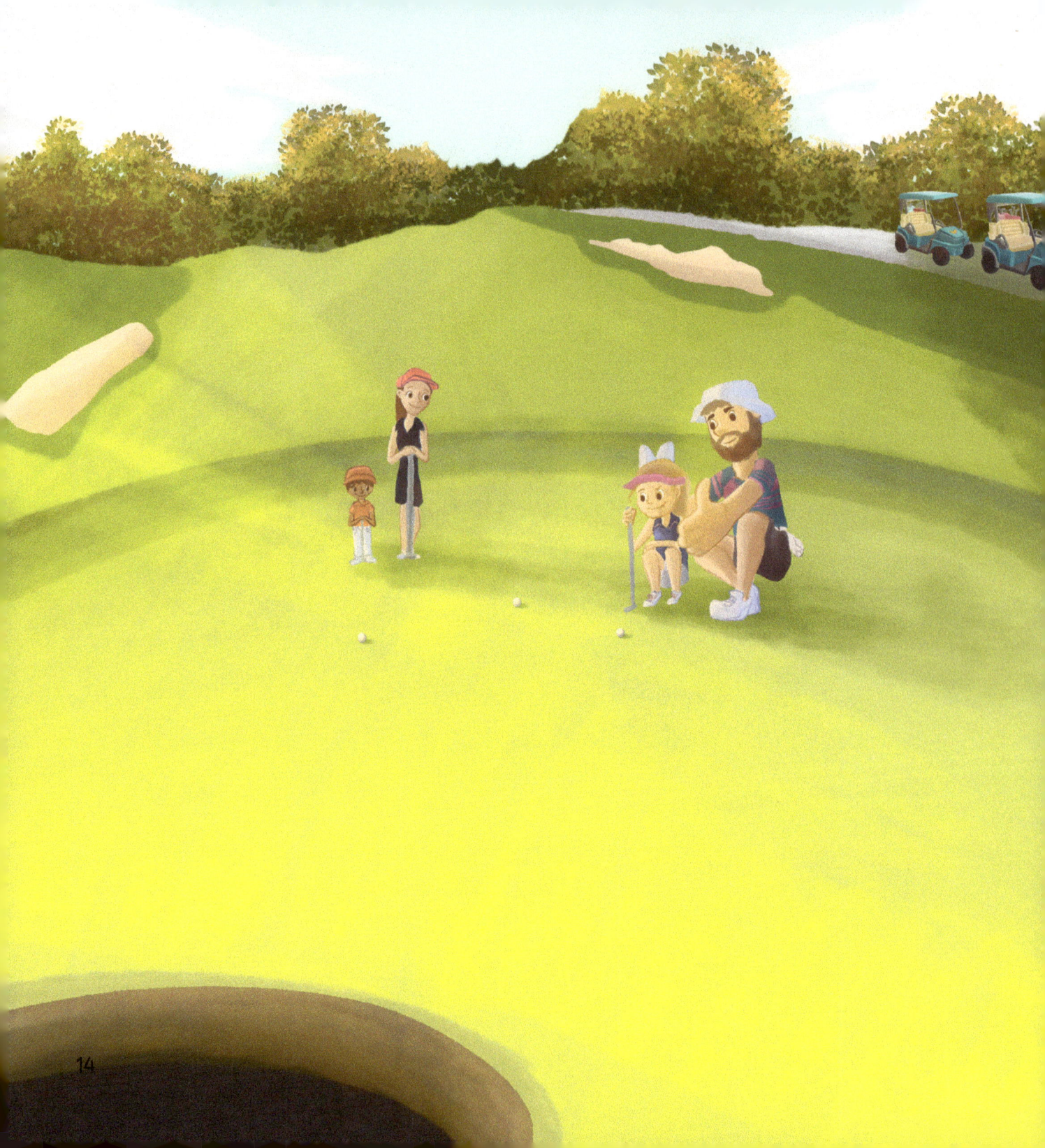

Ella gets on the green!
So close, but so far.
She has a long way to go
if she wants to make par.

Then Ella remembers
what Daddy would say:
"One shot at a time.
That's how you should play."

She takes a hard look.
The ground curves and slopes.
She's trying to see
which way the ball rolls.

Short game is tough.
It's all rhythm and speed.
She asks her Daddy,
"Help me find a good read?"

Ella lines up her putt,
but she makes a mistake.
Her ball misses the hole
and her little heart aches.

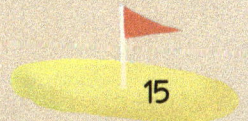

This game is hard.
People practice for years.
Bad breaks will come,
but she must persevere.

Flustered but focused,
Ella steps up to see...
Can she make this next putt
to save her bogey?

The ball goes right in.
Phew! What a relief!
Golf takes endurance,
plus skill and belief.

Now, write down the scores.
There are still holes to play.
Some rules to follow
the rest of the day:

Don't stand too close
to someone swinging a club.
Be ready to play
when your turn finally comes.

Try to be quiet
when a player steps up.
But certainly cheer
when the ball drops in the cup.

There will be good holes and bad.
Do not think of your fears.
Your most useful tool
is right between your ears.

Have lots of fun.
Stay cool under pressure.
Golf brings you joy
and days you will treasure.

Eighteen holes take a toll,
but the day flies by fast!
While her body is tired,
Ella had such a blast!

On to the next round!
She can't wait for more.
And they haven't even stopped
to add up her score.

Ella has a big dream
to be the best of the best.
She must focus, believe,
and work hard in this quest!

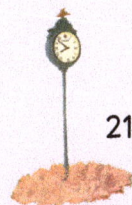

Up at the clubhouse,
they soak in the view.
"This was amazing,"
Ella says in review.

Leo smiles and says,
"What a great practice round!
Time for a tournament.
Think we will be crowned?"

Oh yes! Their next goal!
What fun that would be.
Can they take home first place?
Time to practice and see!

www.ingramcontent.com/pod-product-compliance
Lightning Source LLC
Chambersburg PA
CBHW040850100426
42813CB00015B/2768